AIM HIGH

Irish Sports Stars, Trailblazers and Mavericks

Donny Mahoney
Illustrated by Eoin Coveney

THE O'BRIEN PRESS
DUBLIN

Why Sport Matters

When I was a kid I thought sport was one of the best things in the world – and I still feel the exact same way! We often call our sports stars 'heroes', but where superheroes in comic books and movies may be able to lift boulders or fly through the air thanks to their superpowers, in real life, sportsmen and women rely on their own talent, determination and hard work.

For a small country, Ireland has produced many legends of sport, in many different games. It was so hard to select a final list for this book. In the end, I wanted to tell some of the stories of Irish sport down through the years. But I didn't want to focus only on the country's most talented sportspeople. Greatness in sport is about more than just talent. So this book is about some of Ireland's most extraordinary sportspeople – the great characters who often broke new ground and rewrote the rules of the games they loved. Some of these people are very famous, others deserve to be.

We'll meet Sonia O'Sullivan, the first Irishwoman to win an Olympic medal in athletics, and Brian O'Driscoll, who helped turn Ireland into one of the best rugby countries in the world. We'll also be introduced to Francie Barrett, the first Traveller to box for Ireland in the Olympics, and Iraqi-born Zak Moradi, who won the Lory Meagher Cup with Leitrim. We'll travel back in time to meet the Donegal man who captained the New Zealand rugby team and the Dubliner who became manager of FC Barcelona. And we'll also look to the future, to meet Irish sports trailblazers of tomorrow.

Sport teaches us that we all have the power to change the world. All of these sports stars were kids once. They had hopes and dreams of achieving greatness. With the help of their families and their coaches, their dreams came true. The most important thing is that they all believed in themselves. The odds were against a short lad from the northside of Cork becoming captain of Manchester United. No one would have thought a dressmaker from Dublin could become the world's best female rally driver. But Roy Keane and Rosemary Smith were just two Irish people who believed they could achieve anything in sport if they just worked hard for it. And they're just two of the success stories in this book.

Remember: always aim high, because as these Irish sports stars prove, when you aim high, you can achieve almost anything!

Donny Mahoney, 2020

Contents

Dan Donnelly
Boxing
1788-1820

Dan was born in Dublin in 1788. He had sixteen siblings. Dan's father was a carpenter and everyone thought Dan would be a carpenter too, but he was extremely strong and so instead he became famous in Dublin for his fighting abilities.

A man named William Kelly was on the look-out for an Irish boxer to fight the best fighters in England and prove that the Irish were as tough as their English competitors. William asked Dan to fight one of the best English fighters of the time. Ireland's sporting rivalry with England was as fierce then as it is now. Donnelly's most popular fights came at the Curragh against English fighters. He attracted crowds of up to 20,000 to his fights. His most famous win came in 1815 against the English fighter George Cooper. Dan knocked him out in the 11th round and became a folk hero all around Ireland for his achievement.

Boxing in the 19th century is unrecognisable from the sport we know today. Boxers didn't wear gloves, there weren't many rules and fights went on until a boxer was knocked out. Dan was rumoured to have had the longest arms in the history of boxing; whether or not this is true, he was certainly famed for his punching ability.

He was so famous that after he died, his body was taken by grave robbers and his arm went on to tour the world.

In 2008, Dan was elected to the International Boxing Hall of Fame.

BARRY McGUIGAN & MICHAEL CONLAN

Boxing is a sport where Ireland has consistently 'punched above its weight'. Probably the most beloved Irish boxer of the last fifty years was Monaghan boxer Barry McGuigan. The 'Clones Cyclone' became a symbol of peace at the height of the Troubles in Northern Ireland. His victory over Eusebio Pedroza at Loftus Road in London to win the WBO featherweight title was one of the most memorable evenings in the history of Irish sport.

Michael Conlan is one of the most accomplished fighters Ireland has ever produced. The Belfast fighter won a bronze medal in the 2012 Olympics. He won gold at the 2015 World Championships and seemed destined for a gold medal at the 2016 Olympics in Rio. Sadly, he was defeated in controversial circumstances. Michael turned professional soon after and won the first thirteen fights of his pro career.

Dave Gallaher
Rugby
1873-1917

The New Zealand national rugby team, the All Blacks, have changed the way the game of rugby is played, but not everyone knows that an Irishman was part of the team's early days.

Dave Gallaher was born in Ramelton in County Donegal in 1873. His family were poor farming folk who emigrated to New Zealand when Dave was four. In those days, the boat trip to New Zealand took months, and emigrants rarely returned home. Dave and his family lived in the capital city, Auckland. Dave took up rugby in his new homeland and became one of the best rugby players in the country.

In 1905, the New Zealand national team decided to travel to the Northern Hemisphere to play the national teams of France, England, Ireland, Scotland and Wales, as well as many club sides in each country. This was the first time a New Zealand national side had played outside of the Southern Hemisphere. In those days the teams travelled by boat and had to be away from home for months at a time. Dave, who played on the wing, was selected to captain the New Zealand side.

The New Zealand team attracted huge interest from rugby fans. No one had ever seen the game played this well. They wore a black jersey and black shorts with a white fern on the shirt; journalists invented the term 'All Blacks' to describe them. Unfortunately Dave was injured for New Zealand's visit to Ireland, but 12,000 people at Lansdowne Road saw the All Blacks beat Ireland 15-0. It was the first of many New Zealand wins over Ireland.

Dave's All Blacks team won 34 of 35 games on that tour and finished the tour with 976 points scored and just 59 conceded. The legend of the All Blacks was born! In New Zealand, Dave's team is fondly remembered as 'The Originals' since they were the first All Blacks team.

Dave fought for New Zealand in World War I and died on a Belgian battlefield in 1917.

In 2005, the All Blacks team visited his ancestral home in Ramelton before a game against Ireland, and remembered that famous Tour of 1905. Letterkenny Rugby Club in County Donegal also named their home pitch – the Dave Gallaher Memorial Park – in his honour.

Martin Sheridan
Discus
1881-1918

The *New York Times* once declared that discus thrower Martin Sheridan was 'one of the greatest athletes America has ever known'. In fact, this great American athlete was an Irishman.

Martin was born into a family of seven children in 1881, in Bohola, County Mayo. Even as a young boy he possessed incredible strength. He emigrated to America with two of his brothers in 1899. Martin and his brother Richard joined the New York City police department and in his down time, Martin competed with New York City athletics clubs.

Martin was an incredible all-around athlete. He was brilliant at the long jump, the pole vault, the high jump and the shot put, but his best sport was the discus. He was one of the best athletes in the world in his prime. In Martin's day, the modern Olympics were a new and exciting idea – the first modern Olympic Games were held in 1896. Martin decided to represent the United States in the 1904 Olympics in St Louis, USA. He won the gold medal in the discus. Four years later, the Olympics were held in London. All teams were expected to lower their flag when passing the British king in the royal enclosure, but according to legend, Martin told the US flag bearer not to. 'This flag dips to no earthly king,' he is reported to have said. He won the gold medal in the discus throw and the Greek discus in London.

After the London Olympics, Martin returned to Ireland and carried out demonstrations in Dublin, Dungarvan, Dundalk and Bohola.

'He was the most handsome of the athletes and although he was a giant in size he could run the hundred yards in a little more than ten seconds,' one journalist wrote about Martin.

Sadly, Martin contracted pneumonia and died when he was just thirty-seven years old.

DR PAT O'CALLAGHAN was Ireland's first great Olympian. In the early years of the twentieth century, many of Ireland's international sporting successes came in throwing events in athletics. Dr Pat was no exception. Born in Duhallow, County Cork, he qualified as a surgeon when he was twenty, but he was a fierce sportsman, too. He was especially skilled in the hammer throw. Dr Pat, or 'the Doc' as some called him, won gold in the hammer throw at the 1928 Olympics in Amsterdam. Ireland was a newly-independent country and it was our first-ever gold medal. Dr Pat matched the feat in 1932 in Los Angeles. He was so strong he was even asked to star in a *Tarzan* film!

Multisports

Maeve Kyle

Maeve Kyle was one of the greatest Irish sportspeople of all time. She was Ireland's first female Olympian and Ireland's first triple Olympian. She competed in three different Summer Olympics (1956, 1960 and 1964) in athletics, in three different distances (100m, 200m, and 800m). She also represented Ireland 58 times in hockey and was inducted into the Ireland Hockey Hall of Fame. She was brilliant at swimming, cricket and sailing too.

Liam McHale

The sports of basketball and Gaelic football use a lot of the same skills, but no one has blended them as well as Liam McHale. Born in Ballina, County Mayo, Liam was the best Irish basketball player of his generation. He led his club (Ballina) to two National Cups and six Division 1 titles. At the same time he was starring in the midfield for the Mayo footballers; he represented Mayo from 1985-1999, playing in four All-Ireland finals and winning one All-Star in green and red.

James Cecil Parke

Born in Clones in 1881, James Cecil Parke was brilliant at pretty much every sport he tried. His best sport was probably tennis, where he won the 1912 Australian Open singles and doubles titles. James also won the mixed doubles title at Wimbledon in 1914. In addition he had twenty caps for the Ireland rugby team between 1903 and 1909. In his remarkable sporting career, James represented Ireland in tennis, rugby, cricket, athletics and chess.

Jim Stynes

Another Gaelic footballer who famously switched sports was Jim Stynes. Stynes moved to Australia in 1984 after winning a minor All-Ireland with Dublin to play Australian Rules football. He joined Melbourne Football Club. In 1991, Stynes won the Brownlow medal for 'fairest and best' player in the AFL. He remains the only non-Australian to have won the prize. Stynes was a giant of Aussie Rules football and a statue was erected in his memory outside Melbourne's home ground.

Patrick O'Connell
Footballer and FC Barcelona manager
1887-1959

Patrick O'Connell was a true pioneer of Irish football. He played for and managed football clubs that are now amongst the biggest in the world. Yet, until recently, he was unknown to many Irish football fans.

Paddy, as he was known, was born in Drumcondra in Dublin in 1887. He loved to play football, and was a centre back with Strandville Rovers near Dublin's North Strand. Paddy then joined Belfast Celtic before being offered contracts to play in England. He played with clubs like Sheffield Wednesday and Hull City before transferring to Manchester United. Paddy holds the distinction of being the first Irishman ever to play for Manchester United.

Paddy also captained Ireland during an international career that lasted seven years, winning six caps in the process.

But it is for his achievements as a manager that he is best remembered In 1922, Paddy moved to Spain and began managing some of the most famous clubs in the country. He managed Racing Santander for seven years. The Spanish locals knew him as 'Don Patricio'. He later moved to Real Betis and guided them to their first ever La Liga title. In 1935, Paddy became the first and only Irishman to manage FC Barcelona.

Then, as now, Barcelona was one of the biggest clubs in Spain. But it was not an ideal time to manage them. Back then, the Spanish Civil War was raging. Much of the fighting was happening around Barcelona and the war put FC Barcelona in jeopardy. But luckily, the club was offered a lucrative tour of America. Paddy did a wonderful job leading the tour and Barcelona was able to secure its financial future.

That's why some people refer to Don Patricio as the man who saved FC Barcelona.

Mick Barry
Road Bowling
1919-2014

Road bowling is one of the simplest and most fascinating sports played on this island. While you won't see road bowling on television, it has a passionate following across Ireland.

Road bowling events take place in the countryside, as two competitors throw a metal ball that weighs 28 ounces (793.8 grams) down a country road. A road bowling course is usually around four kilometres in length. Whoever reaches the finish line taking the fewest throws of the bowl is the winner. Fans make bets on which bowler will win and follow them on their journey.

Road bowling has a long-standing connection to rural Co Cork and Armagh, but there are courses in Louth, Limerick, Waterford, Mayo and Wexford. A version of the sport is also played in Germany and the Netherlands. The premier event on the road bowling calendar is the King and Queens of the Road classic, which is held near Midleton, County Cork every October.

It is agreed that Mick Barry of Cork was the greatest road bowler of all time. He was born in the village of Waterfall just outside Cork City. He lived an ordinary life as a groundskeeper at UCC, but he was also an incredible road bowler. In fact, in 1997, he was named Supreme Bowler of the Millennium. Aficionados of the sport called him 'King of the Road'.

Mick played the sport for six decades and was still one of the best bowlers in Ireland when he was in his seventies. He won eight All-Irelands and eleven Munster titles in his legendary career.

'Loft' – how high you can throw the ball – is the most important thing for a successful road bowler and no one could throw the bowl as high as Mick. His greatest achievement as a road bowler came on St Patrick's Day 1955 when he became the first person to ever throw a 16 ounce bowl over Cork's 90 foot tall and 21 foot wide Chetwynd Viaduct. It was a feat of almost superhuman strength. It took fifteen years for someone to equal it.

No one bowled like Mick Barry.

Iris Kellett
Showjumping
1926-2011

Iris Kellett was one of the most extraordinary people ever to compete in the world of Irish showjumping. Iris was small in stature, but she had no fear while on horseback, no matter how big the horse. In her day, showjumping was dominated by male riders. But Iris had no fear of that either.

Iris was born in 1926. Her father was a vet who was also an accomplished horse rider. Iris shared her father's love for horses, and rode in point-to-point races at a young age. After a bad fall during a race, she decided to concentrate on horse jumping.

Aboard her beloved chestnut gelding Rusty, Iris became one of the best showjumpers in Europe in the late 1940s and early 1950s.

Her most important contributions to showjumping were as a coach and a teacher. When she was just a teenager, she ran her family's famous Kellett School of Jumping after her parents fell ill. After her own showjumping career ended, she put her energies back into running the school, and it became one of the best in the world. There, she moulded many of Ireland's best riders. She bred and trained horses and had an amazing ability to develop both a horse and a showjumper into champions. But she wasn't interested in just trophies. She also gave horse-riding lessons to disabled people after she hurt herself badly in a fall and realised how dangerous horse jumping could be.

Iris loved horses and loved horse jumping, and between her own riding, her coaching of world class riders and her work in teaching ordinary people to love horses, she did more for the sport than anyone else in Ireland.

EDDIE MACKEN

Iris's most famous pupil was Eddie Macken, who was one of Ireland's most decorated showjumpers. Eddie was leader of the Irish team when it won the Aga Khan Cup three years in a row from 1977–79. Eddie also won the iconic Hickstead Derby four years in a row from 1976–79.

Most of Eddie's famous wins came aboard the legendary Irish horse Boomerang. Eddie and Boomerang formed a magical partnership, and captured the hearts of the nation. Eddie became a revered figure in world showjumping and represented Ireland in the 1992 and 1996 Summer Olympics.

Christy Ring
Hurling
1920-1979

Christy Ring was more than a hurler. He was a folk hero. According to those who saw him play, no one has hurled like him before or since. He was born in Cloyne, County Cork in 1920 and had four siblings. Christy's father hurled for Cloyne and he used to transport Christy to local hurling matches on the crossbar of his bike.

When Christy was a young boy, there were no underage hurling teams to play for. He practised the game at every opportunity, after Mass and before and after school. His street in Cloyne was called Spit Lane, and just behind it was the town's GAA pitch. It was the perfect place to practise. Christy was very talented and broke through with the Cloyne minors (u18s) when he was just fourteen. He was a member of the Cork team that competed in the 1936 All-Ireland minor hurling final when he was just sixteen. He was still a teenager when he made his senior debut with the Rebel County. By then he had discovered his preferred position: full-forward. Christy was a lethal scorer. He won his first All-Ireland in 1941 – the beginning of a four-in-a-row for his county between 1941 and 1945.

In the 1950s, the rivalry between Cork and Tipperary was at its fiercest and most bitter, and it was Christy's performances against the Premier County that helped turn him into a legend. He was unpredictable and unmarkable.

Christy won eight All-Ireland senior medals and nine Munster medals in his incredible career. He also won fourteen Cork titles with his club Glen Rovers. He scored a total of 33-208 in sixty-five championship appearances for the Rebel County. He played about 1,200 games in his career.

Off the pitch, Christy didn't act like a superstar: he worked driving an oil delivery truck around Cork; to the GAA fans who loved him, he was always known as 'Ringey'.

He retired when he was forty-three years old, after a senior intercounty career spanning twenty-six years. When Christy died in 1979, his funeral in Cork attracted thousands of mourners. His casket was draped in the colours of Glen Rovers and the GAA. Taoiseach Jack Lynch said: 'As long as young men will match their hurling skills against each other on Ireland's green fields … the story of Christy Ring will be told.'

Shay Elliott
Cycling
1934-1971

Ireland has had a long love affair with the sport of cycling. Our twisting country roads are perfect for bicycle racing. It was a young man named Shay Elliott, from Crumlin in Dublin, who put Irish cycling on the world map.

Shay grew up in Dublin playing GAA and did not ride a bike until he was fourteen years old. Yet once he learned to cycle, it was clear that he possessed an extraordinary talent. As a teenager, Shay won a number of amateur races in Ireland and the UK. And though he was training to be a sheet metal worker, he was convinced by professional cyclists to move to France to dedicate his life to his bike. In those days, cycling was one of the biggest sports on the European continent. However, it was dominated by French and Belgian cyclists and it was very difficult for an English speaker like Shay to earn a living as a cyclist.

But that didn't stop him.

In 1955, when he was just twenty-one, Shay became the top-ranked amateur cyclist in all of France. He turned professional two years later and joined the Helyett-Félix Poitin team. Shay broke new ground for Irish cyclists in Europe's biggest races: he was the first English-speaking rider to lead the Giro d'Italia; he finished in third place in the Vuelta a España; in 1963, he led the Tour de France for three days. He spent the majority of his career as a 'domestique' – a rider who helps the team leader by setting the pace or creating a slipstream for the leader to ride in; this is an essential role in a cycling team, but it doesn't come with much glory.

Shay was also one of the first cyclists to speak publicly about the use of drugs in cycling. He deserved more fame in Ireland, but few of his greatest races were televised here. He is revered amongst Ireland's cycling community. Every year, the Shay Elliott memorial race takes place in Wicklow in his honour. The race passes a monument to Shay near Glenmalure, County Wicklow that reads 'In Memory of Shay Elliott, International Racing Cyclist'.

Athletics – Stars of Track

Ronnie Delany

Ronnie Delany may be Ireland's best ever middle-distance runner. His gold medal in the 1500m in the 1956 Summer Olympics in Melbourne remains one of Ireland's greatest sporting moments. At a time when indoor athletics was massively popular in the US, Ronnie was one of the world's best runners and won forty indoor races in a row!

and Field

Eamonn Coghlan

Crumlin's Eamonn Coghlan is one of the most decorated Irish runners of the past fifty years. Nicknamed 'The Chairman of the Boards' (after the indoor running tracks made of wooden boards), Coghlan broke the indoor world record in the 1500m three different times and also won a gold medal in the 5000m in the 1983 World Championships in Helsinki.

Jason Smyth

Despite being legally blind, Jason Smyth is one of the fastest Irishmen of all time. Smyth runs the 100m and 200m and has enjoyed incredible success in the Paralympics. He is a world record holder and won five gold medals in three different Paralympics up to 2016.

Derval O'Rourke

Ireland's most famous runners have all thrived over middle or long distance. Derval O'Rourke, on the other hand, was a powerful hurdler. Derval won gold in 60m hurdles at the 2006 World Indoor Championships, breaking the Irish record in the process. She also won silver at the 2006 and 2010 European championships in the 100m hurdles.

Rosemary Smith
Rally Driving
b. 1937

The sport of motor-racing was dominated by men until Dublin's Rosemary Smith arrived to prove that women have all the talent and guts it takes to compete in rally driving.

Rosemary was born in Dublin in 1937. Her family wanted her to pursue a conventional career in the world of fashion as a dress designer. But Rosemary's father was an amateur car racer, so driving was in her blood. Rosemary was educated by nuns and opened a dressmaking shop in Dublin after school. But she knew her real talent was behind a steering wheel, not a sewing machine! One day in 1959, Delphine Biggar, a female amateur driver, called into Rosemary's dressmaking shop and asked if she would like to attend a rally. Rosemary's career in driving began that day.

Rosemary first started as a co-driver, giving the driver directions. But she quickly transitioned to driving and that's where she made her mark in the sport.

Over her career, Rosemary was viewed as one of the best drivers on the ladies' circuit. She won the Scottish Rally, the Circuit of Ireland Rally, the Alpine Rally in Switzerland and the Acropolis Rally in Greece. In 1965, she became the only woman ever to win the Tulip Rally in Holland. She drove a Hillman Imp and beat a field of male and female drivers to win. She also won the Coupe des Dames at the 1966 Monte Carlo Rally, but the race organisers controversially decided to disqualify Rosemary and nine other drivers.

Rally Driving is, of course, very dangerous. When asked about her relationship with danger, she once replied, 'We don't get on very well. I tumbled down a few mountains.'

When Rosemary test drove a Renault Formula One Sport Car in 2017, aged seventy-nine, she became the oldest person ever to drive an F1 car.

THE DUNLOP FAMILY

The love of motorsports on this island is not restricted to cars. Motorbike rallying is very popular too, especially in Northern Ireland. The most famous family in the Irish motorbike rally scene are the Dunlops.

Joey Dunlop was the most beloved Irish motorcyclist of all time. He won hat-tricks at the famous Isle of Man TT races three times in his fabled career. He was also loved for his charity work for children affected by the war in the Balkans in the 1990s. In 2015, he was voted 'Northern Ireland's Greatest Sports Star'. His brother Robert and his nephews William and Michael were also accomplished motorcyclists. Sadly, the Dunlops know better than anyone just how tragic the sport can be, as Joey, Robert and William all died during races.

Mick O'Connell
Gaelic Football
b. 1937

When sports historians talk about 'pure' Gaelic footballers – the players who embody the ideals of how the game is supposed to be played – they often speak of the great Mick O'Connell of Kerry.

Mick was born in 1937 on Valentia Island, just off the coast of south Kerry and spent most of his life living on the island. His father was a fisherman and Mick himself spent a lot of his childhood in a boat.

Mick gained a love of sport as a child from playing football with Spanish sailors on the island. There was no Gaelic football tradition in his immediate family, but his father bought him a pair of football boots when he was around eleven. Word spread quickly of Mick's football talent and he made his debut with the Kerry seniors in 1956.

There was no bridge connecting Valentia Island to the mainland for most of Mick's intercounty career, and he used to start his trip to training by rowing his own boat to the mainland.

Mick was named Kerry captain for the 1959 Championship when he was only twenty-two. He was determined that Kerry would win an All-Ireland that year, and embarked on a rigorous training regime on the island. Kerry beat Dublin in the 1959 All-Ireland final, but Mick managed to forget the Sam Maguire Cup, leaving it in the Croke Park dressing room. Mick did not go out in Dublin that evening to celebrate. Instead he got a train home from Heuston Station and rowed himself back to Valentia Island.

Mick is seen as the greatest Gaelic football midfielder of all time; people who watched him play said he could leap like a salmon. He was tall and stylish under the high ball and his foot passing was magnificent.

Mick's incredible intercounty career spanned eighteen years. He won four All-Irelands in his senior intercounty career with Kerry.

He was a legendary footballer but he was also very modest: 'Any day if I caught a few good balls and kicked a few good balls that was success,' he said on his eightieth birthday.

George Best
Football
1946-2005

There hadn't been an Irish footballer like George Best before, and there hasn't been one since. He was simply one of the greatest footballers of all time.

George grew up in Belfast and learned the game on the streets of the city; he was a classic street footballer. He was inventive and tricky. Dribbling was his strength. He was a maestro with the ball at his feet.

'Georgie', as many fans called him, was spotted by Manchester United scout Bob Bishop when he was fifteen. Bishop immediately sent a telegram to United manager Matt Busby: 'I think I've found you a genius.' George signed with Manchester United in 1961 and made his first team debut in 1963. He quickly became a sensation. He had long hair and thick sideburns. After United thrashed Benfica in 1966, the Portuguese media called him 'El Beatle', because they thought he looked like a member of the band The Beatles. At a time of great division in Northern Ireland, everyone agreed on the greatness of George Best.

George was voted European Footballer of the Year in 1968, the same year Manchester United won its first European Cup. He was the Messi or Ronaldo of his generation. He was one of the first footballers to be treated like a celebrity, but fame wasn't good for him. He made some bad decisions and battled with alcoholism. He was forced to leave Old Trafford because of his drinking and spent the rest of his career with smaller clubs. He even played in Cork for Cork Celtic.

'We had our problems with the wee fella, but I prefer to remember his genius,' Busby said once. George used to say: 'Pele called me the greatest footballer in the world. That is the ultimate salute to my life.'

LIAM BRADY

People used to think that players from England's top division couldn't do well in the European leagues, but a Dubliner changed all that. Liam Brady moved to London when he was just fifteen to join Arsenal. Liam was an attacking midfielder with a wonderful left foot. He was the first Irish player to be voted PFA Players' Player of the Year, which is a sign of the respect his opponents had for him. After winning the FA Cup in 1979 with Arsenal, Liam joined Juventus in Italy, the biggest club in Serie A. Liam was managed there by future Irish manager Giovanni Trapattoni. In his first season, he scored the penalty that won the Italian league title. In total, Liam played for seven seasons in Serie A.

Anne O'Brien
Football
1956-2016

As women's football finally gets the respect it deserves on a global stage, it's worth remembering the massive contributions that one woman from Dublin made to the game.

Anne O'Brien grew up in Inchicore and got her first pair of football boots when she was around fourteen. Her talent was obvious to everyone and she was asked to play with a team of the best Irish women footballers, known as the All-Stars when she was just seventeen. It was during a game against French club Stade de Reims that French coaches realised what an exceptional talent Anne was. She was a playmaking central midfielder with extraordinary touch.

They offered her a contact. When she accepted, she became the first Irish or British woman ever to play professional football.

Anne won three league titles in three seasons with Stades de Reims. She scored a hat-trick in the 1976 French Cup final. She then moved to Italy to play for Lazio. She won six Italian league titles while playing in Italy, in a career that spanned seven clubs and eighteen years.

Amazingly Anne won only four Ireland caps in her career. Playing professionally outside of Ireland made it difficult for her to play for her country. Her proudest moment in international football came when she was voted 'Player of the Match' in Ireland's 4-1 defeat to France at Parc des Princes in 1973.

Women's football had a very low profile in Ireland at the time, and Anne's achievements in French and Italian football were virtually unknown. So let's give Anne O'Brien the praise that she's long overdue.

STEPHANIE ROCHE

A player who put Irish women's football on the map in more recent times was Stephanie Roche, a skillful striker for Ireland with 50 caps. It was a goal she scored for her club, Peamount United, against Wexford Youths in 2013 that turned her into a global celebrity. It was an incredible goal, she kept the ball up twice with her left foot before volleying in with her right foot from the edge of the penalty box. The goal was uploaded to YouTube and went viral. Stephanie was nominated for the FIFA Puskas award for the best goal scored in world football that year. She finished second in the voting and was photographed beside Messi and Ronaldo at the Ballon d'Or ceremony.

Snooker

Once upon a time, not so long ago, snooker was one of the most popular sports in Ireland and the UK. Over 18 million people tuned in to watch the 1985 World Championship final on television.

At its best, snooker is a game of wonderful skill and high drama. It might look similar to a game of pool because of the table it's played on, but few sports are as mentally demanding as snooker. It's like a game of chess played with a billiards cue. A game of snooker starts with twenty-one billiard balls on the table, each with set scoring values. Each player aims for the highest score in order to win the frame. The finals of the World Championship can last up to 35 frames, spread over two days.

Elite snooker players possess incredible hand-eye coordination and heroic mental strength. Contestants wear bow-ties and waistcoats while playing, which adds to the sport's romance.

Two Irishmen who turned a childhood love of snooker into a lifelong passion were Alex Higgins and Ken Doherty. They had very different playing styles, but both attained greatness in the game.

Belfast's Alex Higgins changed the sport of snooker. He played the game quickly, which earned him the nickname 'Hurricane'. He was described as 'the one true genius that snooker has produced'. He won the World Championship at the Crucible in Sheffield twice in his career, in 1972 and 1982. Alex's flamboyant style of play helped revive the popularity of the sport, as millions tuned in to watch him play. He suffered from gambling and alcohol addiction, but he was a hero to anyone who watched the game of snooker.

Alex was a massive inspiration to the last Irishman to win the World Championship, Ken Doherty. 'He was just a genius,' Ken said of Alex.

Ken learned the game at a snooker hall in Ranelagh in Dublin, near where he grew up. To this day, Ken plays with the same snooker cue that he learned the game with. He was the first snooker player to win both the world amateur and professional title. His win in the 1997 Snooker World Championship at the Crucible was a career-defining moment.

Sonia O'Sullivan
Athletics
b. 1969

Sonia O'Sullivan is one of Ireland's greatest ever sportspeople, one of the greats of distance running, known for her grit and grace. In the 1990s, Sonia's races were national events. It is a sign of how big a star she was that she was known only by her first name: Sonia.

Sonia is from Cobh in Cork. Her dad John was in the Irish navy and played goalkeeper with Cobh Ramblers FC. A talented cross country runner with Ballymore-Cobh AC, Sonia was determined to be an Olympic champion. She finished in ninth place in the 1984 Evening Echo Women's Mini Marathon when she was fifteen. She received a free pair of Adidas and her running career had begun. When she was seventeen, she won both the national junior and senior championships. She was offered a scholarship to run at Villanova University in America, and her career was started to take off.

Sonia was a tall, powerful runner. She had a tremendous kick, which meant she would finish her races with a blistering sprint that her opponents couldn't keep up with.

She was talented at the 1500 metres and the 3000 metres, but her best race was the 5000 metres.

Her dream season came in 1995. She ran twenty-five races that year and finished with twenty-three first place medals. She finished second in the other two races. The highlight of that amazing season came in the 1995 World Championships in Gothenburg, Sweden, where she won the gold medal.

Sonia competed in four different Olympics and won a silver medal in Sydney in 2000. It is the only athletics medal that an Irishwoman has ever won.

Sonia was also a brilliant cross-country runner and won gold medals in the 4km and the 8km in the 1998 World Cross Country Championships in Marrakesh – on the same day!

She has held the Irish record in nine events ranging from 800m to the marathon.

Roy Keane
Football
b. 1971

Roy Keane is known as a warrior, a leader, a fighter, a straight-talker and a legend.

Roy grew up on the north side of Cork City and showed his famous toughness from an early age. He was an exceptional young boxer, but football was his favourite sport. He joined Cork club Rockmount AFC and began to develop his talents as a midfielder.

Roy's Rockmount team went unbeaten for six years in a row. Some of his teammates received offers to play in England, but not Roy. People said he was too small to play at an elite level. Roy wrote letters to many clubs in Britain seeking a trial, but most refused. He wasn't capped for Ireland until he was U16. Still, Roy remained fiercely determined to make it as a footballer.

In 1989, Roy signed with Cobh Ramblers in the League of Ireland. It was while playing for Cobh that Keane was spotted by Nottingham Forest scout Noel McCabe. Keane impressed Forest legendary manager Brian Clough during his trial and was soon offered a professional contract.

In 1993, Roy broke the English transfer record when he joined Manchester United. His arrival at Old Trafford heralded a golden era for the club. With Alex Ferguson as manager, Roy captained a United team featuring an amazing generation of academy players like David Beckham, Ryan Giggs and Paul Scholes. Manchester United dominated the Premiership for twenty years and Roy was their heart and soul.

Roy had a motto: 'fail to prepare, prepare to fail'. He could be a bit scary, but he gave everything of himself, and expected the same in return.

Roy had a memorable career playing for Ireland. He played in every game for Ireland at the 1994 World Cup. Eight years later, he inspired Ireland to qualify for the 2002 World Cup. Unfortunately, tensions with manager Mick McCarthy spilled over during Ireland's World Cup training camp on the island of Saipan, and Roy Keane left the squad before the tournament. 'Saipan' will be forever remembered as the biggest controversy in Irish sporting history.

After his playing career, Roy has worked as a manager and as a pundit. He also been a longtime ambassador for Irish Guide Dogs for the Blind. Beneath the prickly exterior, Roy has proven himself to have a heart of gold.

Stars of Golf

Some of the world's most beautiful and challenging golf courses are in Ireland. So it's not surprising that this island has created its fair share of legendary golfers. Golf is played all over the planet, with golfers travelling around the world to play at important tournaments like The Open and the Ryder Cup, which are held on different courses each year.

Shane Lowry

Shane Lowry is one of the most beloved Irish sportspeople of recent times. He grew up in Clara, County Offaly and was an accomplished pitch and putt player as a child. He won the Irish Open as an amateur in 2009. There were massively emotional scenes in Portrush in 2019 when Shane won the first Open on Irish soil since 1951.

Rory McIlroy

Rory McIlroy is undoubtedly Ireland's best ever golfer. He was a child prodigy. He was just twenty-two when he won the 2011 US Open at Congressional. McIlroy also won two PGAs and one Open by the time he was thirty. He also contributed to four Ryder Cup winning teams for Europe.

Stephanie Meadow

Stephanie Meadow is one of Ireland's best young female golfers. Stephanie grew up in County Tyrone. She moved to America, aged thirteen, to chase her dream of being a pro golfer. She finished in third place in the US Open, her first pro tournament. Stephanie also represented Ireland in the 2016 Olympics and, as of 2020, had two professional wins.

Padraig Harrington

Padraig Harrington was the first golfer from the Republic of Ireland to win a major. In a span of two years, he won The Open twice – at Carnoustie and Royal Birkdale – and the PGA Championship at Oakland Hills. He was also an accomplished Ryder Cup player and was selected to captain Europe for the 2020 Ryder Cup.

Anthony 'AP' McCoy
National Hunt Racing
b. 1974

There has never been a jockey with the work ethic and determination of Anthony Peter McCoy, or 'AP' as his many fans call him.

AP was born in 1974 and grew up in Moneyglass, County Antrim. Many people thought he was too tall to be a jockey, but he didn't listen to them. When he was only fifteen, he left home to move to Carlow to train as a jockey for trainer Jim Bolger. He rode his first winner when he was seventeen years old. Soon after, he moved to England, and quickly established himself as one of the most reliable jumps jockeys in Ireland or Britain.

AP was famous for his toughness. Over his career, he broke bones in his spine, both shoulder blades, both collarbones, ribs, an ankle, cheekbones, a wrist and a leg, as well as dislocating his thumb and chipping teeth. But AP was relentless in his pursuit of greatness. His statistics were staggering. When he retired in 2015, he'd had 4,357 wins. He had been champion jockey for twenty years in a row. It's impossible to imagine another jockey matching those records. How did he do it? He raced day in and day out, all over the UK and Ireland.

AP rode horses for legendary racehorse owner JP McManus during some of the most successful parts of his career. AP won every big event in racing, but his most cherished win came when he rode 'Don't Push It' to victory in the 2010 Grand National. It was his fifteenth time to try to win the world's most famous horse race. He was the first jockey ever to be named 'BBC Sports Personality of the Year'.

RUBY WALSH & RACHAEL BLACKMORE
Ruby Walsh was one of AP McCoy's great rivals. He was born into a great racing family in Kildare – his dad Ted and his sister Katie were also involved in the sport. While AP was a more consistent winner, Ruby was a rider for the big occasion. He had 59 winners at Cheltenham Festival, with his two Gold Cup wins on Kauto Star in 2007 and 2009 the stuff of horse-riding legend.

Rachael Blackmore is one of the best jockeys in the UK or Ireland riding today. She is certainly the most successful female jockey ever. From Killenaule, County Tipperary, she was the first female to ride professionally in thirty years. Rachael had two wins at the 2019 Cheltenham Festival and finished second place in the race to be the Champion Jockey that year.

Francie Barrett
Boxing
b. 1977

Ireland has a proud boxing tradition and, over the decades, the Travelling community has made a massive contribution to the sport. However, it took the rise of a Galway boxer named Francie Barrett during the 1996 Olympics for Ireland to finally recognise exactly what Travellers had brought to Irish sport.

Francie Barrett grew up on a Galway halting site. He was the third child in a family of eleven. At the time, Travellers weren't accepted in boxing clubs in Galway, so Francie and his brothers had to train inside shipping containers on the outskirts of the city.

Francie was trained by a barber named Chick Gillen who had been a Connacht boxing champion. There were no 'high performance units' for Francie to train with, but he was a brilliant 'southpaw', or left-handed boxer, and qualified for the 1996 Summer Olympics in Atlanta in the light welterweight division when he was just nineteen. In doing so, he became the first Traveller to represent Ireland at the Olympic Games.

Francie carried the tricolour into the Olympic stadium during the Opening Ceremonies. At those same Olympics, legendary boxer Muhammad Ali lit the Olympic torch. It was a landmark moment for Irish Travellers, who had to deal with many disadvantages compared to the rest of Irish society.

During the 1996 Summer Games, Francie hammered Brazilian opponent Zely Fereira dos Santos 32-7 in his first fight. Unfortunately, he was defeated by a Tunisian fighter in the Round of 16, which ended his dream of winning an Olympics medal. But Francie returned to Ireland as a national hero and was given an open-top bus parade when he returned to Galway.

ANDY LEE & JOHN JOE NEVIN

Other Travellers have followed in Francie's footsteps, like Andy Lee from Limerick and John Joe Nevin from Mullingar. Andy represented Ireland in the 2004 Olympics in Athens and later became the first Traveller to win a world title when he won the WBO middleweight title. John Joe was the first Traveller to win an Olympic medal – he won silver at the 2012 Olympics. John Joe was famous for his quick feet; his 'Mullingar Shuffle' often confused opponents.

Brian O'Driscoll
Rugby
b. 1979

You can divide the history of the Irish rugby into two eras: before Brian O'Driscoll and after Brian O'Driscoll.

Before Brian made his Ireland debut in 1999, Irish rugby players battled bravely, but didn't often win. By the time he retired in 2014, Ireland had joined the ranks of the world's elite.

Brian grew up in Clontarf in north Dublin. His parents were both doctors. He grew up in a rugby-mad household, but he also played Gaelic football. Brian went to Blackrock College and played on the 'Dream Team' that won the 1996 Senior Cup. With five future Irish internationals that team was seen as the greatest Irish schools rugby team of all time.

Back then, Brian's rugby skills were still developing: he was only Blackrock's sub scrum half. But he was selected for the Ireland U19s, and it became clear that he had rare skills. Brian earned his first Ireland cap when he was just nineteen. Only a year later, he scored a hat-trick in the Stade de France as Ireland beat France in Paris for the first time since 1972.

Brian played outside centre. He was a genius with the ball in his hand as well as a masterful defender. In 2003, Brian became the youngest-ever Ireland captain.

His best season came in 2009, when he inspired Ireland to its first Grand Slam victory since 1947. That same season, he led Leinster to its first-ever European Cup.

Brian also played on four Lions tours and he was captain of the 2005 tour of New Zealand. He retired as the all-time leading try scorer in the history of the Six Nations with twenty-six tries and is seen as one of the greatest rugby players of the past fifty years.

NIAMH BRIGGS

Niamh Briggs was front and centre when the Irish women's team made their big breakthrough in rugby. Waterford-woman Niamh played Gaelic football with the Waterford senior team, but rugby was her best sport and she made her Ireland debut in 2008 against France. Full back was her preferred position, but she also played out half. 2013 was a landmark for Irish women's rugby, and Niamh was a huge part of that. That year, Ireland beat England for the first time, and won their first-ever Grand Slam, Triple Crown and Six Nations. Niamh finished top scorer in the Six Nations that year. She was also instrumental in Ireland's win over New Zealand in the 2014 Rugby World Cup, kicking two conversions and a penalty as Ireland prevailed 17-14. This was the first time an Ireland senior team had ever beaten New Zealand.

Cora Staunton
Gaelic Football
b. 1981

It's not enough to call Cora Staunton the greatest women's Gaelic footballer of all time. Her place in the game is bigger than that. She has changed the way a lot of Irish people think about female athletes.

Cora grew up in Carnacon, County Mayo. She was the second in a family of seven. She was brilliant at Gaelic football from a young age. She was so good she played with the local boys' team. At just fourteen, Cora played in her first Mayo senior Championship game and she scored 0-10.

She was invited to a trial for the Ireland U16 football team, but she said no. She preferred to be a Mayo footballer.

Cora was a towering presence. She had tremendous power in front of goal. She is the LGFA's all-time leading scorer. In sixty-six Championship appearances for Mayo, she scored fifty-nine goals and 476 points. By comparison, in 2019, her countyman Cillian O'Connor broke the men's all-time scoring record by scoring 23-285. Cora scored at least 300 points more!

Cora won her first All-Ireland with Mayo in 1999; she played for only ninety seconds as a ceremonial gesture as she'd broken her collarbone in training.

She won with Mayo again in 2002, when they beat Waterford. In all, Cora won four All-Irelands with Mayo and was chosen for eleven All Stars. She won another six All-Irelands with her club Carnacon.

Cora was talented in many sports beyond GAA and football. She was also a very good rugby player, and in 2017 she was the first international player selected to play in the brand-new women's Aussie Rules – which is very like Gaelic football – league. She was drafted by the Greater Western Sydney Giants and moved to Australia to play with them. She scored eleven goals in fourteen games and by the start of the 2020 season, seventeen other Irishwomen had followed in Cora's footsteps and joined the Australian Football League.

Cora is a true trailblazer.

Katie Taylor
Boxing
b. 1986

Ireland has won more Olympic medals in boxing than in any other sport. There are so many legendary fighters from this island; of them all, Katie Taylor is arguably Ireland's greatest boxer.

Katie grew up in Bray, County Wicklow. She was trained by her dad Pete, who was a former Irish amateur boxing champion. Her two brothers, Lee and Peter, also boxed. As a girl growing up, she had to fight against boys because there were no girls to box. She won the first legally sanctioned woman's fight in Ireland when she was fifteen years old.

Katie's record as an amateur boxer was incredible. She was World Champion five times. Between 2005 and 2016 she lost only four fights.

Boxing wasn't an Olympic sport for women when Katie was coming up through the ranks, but she campaigned tirelessly to get women's boxing into the Olympic Games.

Eventually women's boxing was admitted into the 2012 Summer Olympics in London. Katie trained for those Olympics in a gym in Bray with no women's toilet or shower. But that didn't stop her. She won a gold medal in the middleweight division, in front of a rapturous crowd filled with Irish people. It was one of the most famous days in Irish sport; the very first year that women's boxing was at the Olympics, it was a source of great national pride that an Irishwoman won an Olympic gold medal.

Katie turned pro four years later and quickly went about winning all the Championship belts she could. When she defeated Delfine Persoon in June 2019, she became the undisputed world lightweight champion. That same year, she was voted 'best pound for pound' boxer in the world.

If it wasn't for boxing, Katie might be best remembered for her abilities as a football player. She won the FAI Women's Cup with Peamount FC and won eleven international caps with Ireland between 2006 and 2009.

KELLIE HARRINGTON

Katie is not Ireland's only successful female boxer. Kellie Harrington has had her own share of success. Kellie grew up in Portland Row in inner-city Dublin. She left school in second year. When she joined the Corinthians boxing club at sixteen, she found her purpose in life. After winning a number of European medals, Kellie had her first major breakthrough in 2016, when she won a silver medal at the World Championships in the light welterweight division. She also won a gold medal in the lightweight division at the 2018 World Championships in New Delhi, India.

Eoin Morgan
Cricket
b. 1986

When England dramatically beat New Zealand to win the 2019 Cricket World Cup, it was also a landmark moment for Irish cricket. That's because the captain of the England team was a Dubliner. His name was Eoin Morgan.

Eoin was born in Rush in north county Dublin. He came from a family of six siblings. He was practically born with a cricket bat in his hand. Eoin's father was Irish, his mother was English and he grew up with passports for both countries. The area was a hot bed for cricket, and Eoin was a stand-out star with Rush Cricket Club from a young age.

Cricket in Ireland had been in the doldrums for decades, but Eoin's generation helped revive the sport. Eoin was part of the Ireland squad that helped put cricket on the map at the 2007 Cricket World Cup, and his team would go on to shock mighty Pakistan in that tournament.

A few years later, Eoin was asked to transfer to play for England, one of the best teams in world cricket, and he couldn't say no. At the time, Ireland did not have Test cricket status and could not play a full schedule of games in a year. Eoin did really well with England, particularly in One Day Internationals (ODIs). Eoin was named England captain for the 2015 World Cup but his greatest success came four years later when England won the World Cup on home soil. The final against New Zealand at Lords was one of the most dramatic games of cricket ever played. After England won in a Super Over, Eoin stepped forward to lift the World Cup trophy.

It was a massive day for English cricket, but it couldn't have happened without this Irishman.

Easkey Britton
Surfing
b. 1987

As an island nation in the north Atlantic, Ireland is the perfect place to learn to surf. The waters off Ireland might not be as warm as those in Hawaii or Bali, but the waves are perfect.

One of the best surfers to emerge from Ireland in the past thirty years is Easkey Britton, who was named after the small north Sligo surfing village of Easkey.

Easkey's grandmother Mary ran a hotel near the beautiful Donegal seaside town of Rossnowlagh. After a trip to California, she was determined to bring two surfboards back for hotel guests to use. Easkey's dad Barry learned to surf on those surfboards, and he and his brothers became surfing pioneers in Ireland.

Easkey was taught to surf at age four by her father and has spent much of her life on a surfboard. When she was young, competitive surfing was dominated by men, but Easkey won the national woman's title five times in a row, as well as the British tour championship.

She was the first woman to ride the famous 'big wave' near the Cliffs of Moher off Doolin, which is viewed as one of the biggest waves in the world.

Easkey was the first woman to be nominated for the Global WSL Big Wave Awards for a ride of a wave at Mullaghmore in Sligo. She was also the first woman to surf in Iran. When she's not catching waves, she works as a scientist and academic.

ELLEN KEANE – SWIMMING
We have always had a fondness for water sports here in Ireland, and Ellen Keane is one of the most inspiring Irish swimmers ever – though her left arm was undeveloped at birth, that didn't stop Ellen from becoming an elite swimmer.
Ellen was Ireland's youngest-ever Paralympian when she swam for Ireland at age thirteen at the 2008 Beijing Paralympics. She had a disappointing London Paralympics, but then won bronze for Ireland in the 100m breaststroke in Rio. Ellen has spoken publically about how she learned to embrace and love her differences.

Zak Moradi

Hurling

b. 1990

The GAA has served up many incredible stories since its foundation, but perhaps nothing as incredible as an Iraqi-born Leitrim hurler winning silverware at Croke Park. That's the amazing story of Leitrim hurler Zak Moradi.

Semaco (Zak) Moradi was born in 1990 in Ramadi in central Iraq. His family was Iranian-Kurdish. In 2003, America invaded his country and Zak's family had to flee their homeland. Zak's brother worked for the UN and helped them relocate to Ireland. The Moradis settled in Carrick-on-Shannon, County Leitrim, where local hurler Clement Cunniffe introduced Zak to the sport of hurling when he did skills demonstration in school one day. Learning to play hurling didn't just help Zak learn English, it helped him assimilate into Irish culture. The Moradi family moved to Dublin when he was fifteen. It was there he picked up the nickname Zak. He maintained his links to Leitrim and made his debut with the Leitrim hurlers in 2010.

Leitrim was hardly a hurling stronghold, but they competed fiercely in the Lory Meagher Cup in recent years. Leitrim reached the 2019 Lory Meagher Cup final against Lancashire. Zak and his one-time mentor Clement were now teammates. It was a thrilling final that went to extra time. Zak started the match on the bench but came on to score a glorious point when the match was in added time. Leitrim won the match by a point and Zak became the first Iraqi-born hurler to head up the steps of the Hogan Stand to win a GAA medal.

THE GAA MELTING POT

The GAA has always reflected Irish society. For much of its history, its members were mostly from Irish backgrounds. But as Ireland opened its door to cultures from all over the world, the complexion of the GAA has changed. There have been a number of top intercounty players with immigrant backgrounds. Wexford's Lee Chin has a Chinese father and an Irish mother. He won an All-Star in 2019 and became one of Ireland's best hurlers. In Gaelic football, Mayo's Shairoze Akram is believed to be the first Pakistani-born player to play intercounty football. He won an U21 All-Ireland with Mayo in 2016. Liberian-born Boidu Sayeh has established himself as a regular in the Westmeath team. 'Ireland is a place now that is so multicultural, it's normal to be different,' Lee said. And he's right!

O'Donovan Brothers
ROWING
b. 1992 & 1994

For two weeks in 2016, Gary and Paul O'Donovan turned rowing into one of the most popular sports in Ireland. Their heroic rowing and hilarious interviews made them into national celebrities during the 2016 Summer Olympics.

Gary and Paul grew up in the parish of Aughadown outside Skibbereen, in West Cork. Their father Teddy was a rower and coached Gary and Paul at Skibbereen Rowing Club. A beautiful town right on the water, Skibbereen is a perfect place to learn to row, but unlike their competitors from other countries, the brothers did not have incredible training facilities to work with. However, through sheer hard work, they became two of the best rowers in the world. They also credit their granny, Mary, for the soup and brown bread she fed them after training sessions!

Gary and Paul were brilliant rowers from an early age, and won a gold medal in junior quad sculls in 2008 in one of the UK's top regattas. They had many successes in their young careers, but it wasn't until the 2016 Olympics that the brothers became household names. They won the hearts of the nation with their tremendous performance on the water, and their brilliant interviews off it.

They explained their tactics for success in rowing: 'Close your eyes and pull like a dog'. They credited their success to a pre-race meal of 'steak and spuds'. They were sports stars who spoke like regular Irish people.

In the end, they won a silver medal in the lightweight double skulls. It was the first time Ireland had ever won a medal in rowing in the Olympics. They did it by being themselves, the Skibbereen way.

ANNALISE MURPHY

Most people in Ireland hadn't heard of the sport laser radial until Rathfarnham sailor Annalise Murphy came along in 2012. Her goal was to become the first Irish person since David Wilkins and James Wilkinson in 1980 to win an Olympic medal in sailing for Ireland. She was desperately unlucky not to win a medal in the 2012 Summer Olympics, finishing in fourth place overall. Annalise had four years to train, and she did not disappoint by the time the Rio Olympics came around. She finished in second place, and became the first Irish woman to win a medal in sailing.

The Irish Women's Hockey Team

In just two years, the Irish women's hockey team broke so much new ground for Irish women's team sports. It all began at the 2018 Hockey World Cup in London. Ireland entered the competition ranked sixteenth in the world – the lowest-ranked team in the tournament. The Irish team were part-time players – they all had to work in other jobs as well as playing hockey. No one gave them a fighting chance. But it was a crazy summer, as a heatwave swept Ireland. And the Irish team went on a red hot run.

Ireland beat the USA and India in the group phase of the tournament. Then they won the quarterfinal over India and the semifinal over Spain in penalty shootouts. Ireland's star performer was goalkeeper Ayeisha McFerran. The native of Larne, County Antrim was like a brick wall between the posts. She made heroic save after heroic save.

Ireland then advanced to the final against the number one ranked team in the world, the Netherlands. Ireland lost the game 6-0, but won the hearts of the whole country. Afterwards McFerran was named Goalkeeper of the Tournament.

The hockey team was involved in even more dramatics just a year later. Ireland had to beat Canada in a playoff to reach the Olympics for the first time ever. The teams played two entire matches without scoring a goal, so it would again take penalties to decide the winner. Ireland fell behind initially, only to seize the momentum back when Róisín Upton scored a penalty despite having a broken bone in her wrist. That goal forced sudden death penalties. Ayeisha then made a save to seal qualification, and Ireland had booked a trip to Tokyo.

They were the first Irish women's hockey team ever to qualify for the Olympics, and their success will inspire generations of hockey players to come.

The Dublin Five-in-a-Row Team

The 'Five in a Row' (winning the All-Ireland Final five years in a row) is the greatest team achievement in men's intercounty GAA. Few thought it could be done. No team had ever done it in Gaelic football or hurling, until Dublin came along and completed the unbelievable feat in 2019.

It's hard to believe now but Dublin had earned a reputation for underperforming. Between 1984 and 2010, they won just one All-Ireland final. But the tide turned in 2011 under manager Pat Gilroy. That year, Dublin beat Kerry in the All-Ireland, thanks to an injury-time free from goalkeeper Stephen Cluxton. The rest, as they say, is history.

Stephen was the heart of this great Dublin team. He made his Dublin debut in 2001 and, over time, transformed the goalkeeper position. His brilliant kickouts gave Dublin their platform for attack. He was also a tremendous shot stopper. The Dubs were gifted with legendary players in every key section of the field. Whether it was Bernard Brogan's scoring ability, Dean Rock's free taking, Brian Fenton's power in the midfield or Philly McMahon's rugged defending, Dublin proved almost impossible to stop. Mayo ran them close in the 2013, 2016 and 2017 All-Irelands, but Dublin always found a way to win. In September 2019, Dublin overcame Kerry in a replay to win that famous five-in-a-row.

Guiding them was calm and modest Jim Gavin, who amazingly lost only one Championship game in seven remarkable years in management.

Dublin dominated the decade of the 2010s, winning seven All-Ireland's in nine years. They can say they're the best Gaelic football team of all time, and that's saying something.

Rising Stars

Mona McSharry

Sligo has not produced many champion swimmers but Mona McSharry is changing that. Mona's best race is the backstroke and she broke the Irish record in four different races before she even turned 20.

Boidu Sayeh

Boidu moved to Ireland from war-torn Liberia when he was eight years old. He had no idea what Gaelic football was, but he picked the game quickly in Moate. He established himself in the Westmeath senior team before turning twenty-two and seems certain to be a stalwart for them over the next decade.

Rhys McClenaghan

Ireland has very little history with the sport of gymnastics, so the success of County Down's Rhys McCleneghan in the pommel horse is truly extraordinary. Rhys won the silver medal in the 2019 World Championships and seems destined for Olympic greatness in the sport.

Troy Parrott

Troy Parrott is the brightest Irish football prospect since Robbie Keane. After playing with the Belvedere Club in Dublin, Troy signed with Spurs and was handed his Premier League debut with Spurs at just seventeen. Weeks later, He won his first Ireland senior cap, when Ireland played New Zealand

Rhasidat Adeleke

Rhasidat Adeleke may be the woman to deliver Ireland's first real success in Olympic sprinting. The Tallaght sprinter won gold in the 100m in the 2019 Youth Olympics and a gold medal in the 200m in the European U18 championships.

Beibhinn Parsons

Beibhinn's skill on the rugby pitch was obvious at an early age. The Ballinasloe winger was the youngest player ever to be capped for Ireland when she won her first cap at sixteen in 2019. She was a stalwart of Ireland's 2020 Six Nations, scoring two tries.

About the Author

DONNY MAHONEY is a writer and journalist. He was born in America and has lived in Ireland since 2004. He is one of the co-founders of the website Balls.ie, where he works today.

About the Illustrator

EOIN COVENEY is an Irish illustrator who has worked extensively in advertising, comics, books, magazines and other media in Ireland and internationally.

First published 2020 by
The O'Brien Press Ltd.
12 Terenure Road East,
Rathgar, Dublin 6, D06 HD27, Ireland.
Tel: +353 1 4923333; Fax: +353 1 4922777
E-mail: books@obrien.ie; Website: www.obrien.ie
The O'Brien Press is a member of Publishing Ireland.

ISBN: 978-1-78849-208-9

10 9 8 7 6 5 4 3 2 1
24 23 22 21 20

Printed and bound in Poland by Białostockie Zakłady Graficzne S.A.
The paper in this book is produced using pulp from managed forests.

Published in:
DUBLIN
UNESCO
City of Literature